SHARK SEARCH

In Search of
Whale Sharks

Caitie McAneney

PowerKiDS
press

New York

Published in 2016 by The Rosen Publishing Group, Inc.
29 East 21st Street, New York, NY 10010

First Edition

Editor: Caitie McAneney
Book Design: Mickey Harmon

Photo Credits: Cover, p. 1 (iron bars) Wayne Lynch/All Canada Photos/Getty Images; cover, pp. 1, 3, 4, 6, 8, 10, 12, 14, 16, 18, 20–24 (background) Ase/Shutterstock.com; cover (whale shark) Andrea Izzotti/Shutterstock.com; pp. 5, 7 (main), 19, 20, 22 Krysztof Odziomek/Shutterstock.com; p. 7 (inset) Nazir Erwan Amin/Shutterstock.com; pp. 9, 11 Dudarev Mikhail/Shutterstock.com; p. 13 (inset) https://upload.wikimedia.org/wikipedia/commons/2/28/Copepodkils.jpg; p. 13 (main) Amanda Nicholls/Shutterstock.com; p. 15 Rich Carey/Shutterstock.com; p. 17 alain pardon/Shutterstock.com.

Library of Congress Cataloging-in-Publication Data

McAneney, Caitie, author.
 In search of whale sharks / Caitie McAneney.
     pages cm. — (Shark search)
 Includes index.
 ISBN 978-1-5081-4351-2 (pbk.)
 ISBN 978-1-5081-4352-9 (6 pack)
 ISBN 978-1-5081-4353-6 (library binding)
 1. Whale shark—Juvenile literature. 2. Sharks—Juvenile literature. I. Title.
 QL638.95.R4M43 2016
 597.3'3—dc23
                              2015028131

Manufactured in the United States of America

CPSIA Compliance Information: Batch #BW16PK: For Further Information contact Rosen Publishing, New York, New York at 1-800-237-9932

Contents

A Gentle Giant

When you think of a shark, you probably think of sharp teeth, surprise attacks, and a thirst for blood. However, there are plenty of gentle sharks, and the biggest of those is the whale shark.

Whale sharks look a lot like whales because of their size and shape. However, whales can't breathe underwater because they're **mammals**. Whale sharks have **gills** to breathe underwater because they're actually fish. In fact, the whale shark is the largest fish in the ocean!

Luckily for us, this huge shark would never hunt a person. They're happy eating tiny sea creatures instead.

Big Bodies

The easiest way to **identify** a whale shark is by looking at its size. On average, whale sharks are 18 to 33 feet (5.5 to 10 m) long. The largest whale shark ever measured was 40 feet (12 m) long. That's bigger than most school buses!

You can also identify a whale shark by its markings. Whale shark skin has different shades of color, from gray to blue to brown on top, and white on its underside. These sharks also have a pattern of lines and dots on their back.

Scientists aren't sure why whale sharks have patterned skin. Some think whale sharks may have **evolved** from spotted carpet sharks that live on the ocean floor.

carpet shark

Weird Teeth

Have you ever held a shark tooth? Many sharks have rows of sharp teeth for hunting. The whale shark has lots of teeth, too. Whale sharks can have more than 4,000 of them! The teeth are arranged in about 300 rows. However, each tooth is very tiny. It's smaller than a grain of rice, and it's curved like a tiny claw.

Whale sharks have a flat head and huge jaws. They open their mouth wide to catch **prey**.

Whale sharks like to feed close to the surface of the water. Their wide mouth catches many tiny creatures.

Where Do Whale Sharks Live?

If you're on a shark search, it's best to know the places sharks call home. Whale sharks can be found in most oceans around the world. They like tropical, or warm, waters best. They like to swim in the open sea.

Some whale sharks **migrate** to the central west coast of Australia each year. That's because there are lots of plankton in a **coral reef** there. Scientists think whale sharks migrate farther and more often than we know.

If you want to spot a whale shark, visit Australia's Ningaloo Reef. You can go **snorkeling** to meet these amazing animals.

11

Huge Hunters

Zooplankton are tiny creatures, such as krill and arrow worms, that float in ocean waters. They may be tiny, but they're a whale shark's favorite meal.

When a whale shark senses a school of plankton, it opens its mouth wide. Then, it pushes its jaws forward and sucks in water. The shark moves its head like a vacuum from side to side to suck in as much plankton as possible. Then, the whale shark closes its mouth, and the plankton are officially dinner.

The water in the whale shark's mouth flows out its gills, but the plankton are left behind in its mouth. This is known as filter feeding.

zooplankton

Smelling for Prey

Plankton aren't the only items on a whale shark's menu. They also like tiny ocean creatures such as small fish and **crustaceans**.

When hunting, a whale shark needs to rely on its sense of smell. That's because its eyes are located on the sides of the head. Also, its eyes are small, so its sight isn't very sharp. Once the whale shark locates its food by smell, it can open its mouth wide and eat all it wants.

You might think a giant fish would hunt large ocean animals. However, plankton are so small people can barely see them!

Baby Whale Sharks

Can you imagine a huge whale shark as a tiny baby? Even though whale sharks grow to huge sizes, they start out life quite small. Whale shark babies, or pups, are only about 21 inches (53 cm) long. A mother whale shark carries hundreds of eggs inside her body. Only some of the eggs become pups.

The massive mother carries the eggs until the babies are ready. Then she gives birth to live pups, which can number in the hundreds. The mother leaves her pups to take care of themselves.

Most fish lay eggs, but whale sharks give birth to live pups.

17

Whale Sharks in Danger

Can you imagine any animal hunting this giant shark? Young whale sharks have to watch out for big fish, including other sharks. However, an adult whale shark is lucky that no other animal is big enough to fight it. Because of that, it has no natural predators.

People are the only real enemy of the whale shark. Some people hunt these gentle giants for their fins, while others hunt them for their meat. Some people kill whale sharks for the oil in their liver.

Whale sharks are vulnerable, which means their populations are at risk of falling. If populations dip too low, the **species** could be at risk of dying out.

Keeping Whale Sharks Safe

People have a great responsibility to keep whale sharks alive for many years to come. However, whale sharks are overfished in some places, especially parts of Asia. In the Philippines, it's now against the law to fish for whale sharks. Laws like this can keep whale sharks safe.

Right now, the whale shark is still a mystery. It's hard to find and study. However, the more people know about this big fish, the more care they may take to keep it safe.

Tourism has grown in some places because of whale sharks there. People who dive to meet whale sharks need to be careful. They shouldn't chase or hurt these animals in any way.

Shark Bites!

 A whale shark's throat is only about the size of a quarter.

 A whale shark can weigh 20 tons (18 mt) or more.

 Whale sharks are slow swimmers at only about 2.3 miles (3.7 km) per hour while feeding.

 In 1925, there was a report of a whale shark 60 feet (18 m) long.

 The pattern of spots around a whale shark's gills is like a human's fingerprint—no two patterns are alike.

 A whale shark's mouth can stretch to over 3 feet (0.9 m) wide.

A Friendly Fish

Whale sharks are the gentle giants of the ocean. They aren't like other sharks, such as great whites and tiger sharks, which sometimes attack humans. In fact, these sharks couldn't eat a person even if they wanted to. Their throat is far too small!

These large, friendly fish mind their own business, and it's important that people do the same. It's okay to dive with a whale shark, but remember: these huge sharks deserve a huge amount of respect.

Glossary

coral reef: The hard remains of coral animals that form a line in ocean waters.

crustacean: An animal with a hard shell, jointed limbs, feelers, and no backbone.

evolve: To grow and change over time.

gill: The body part that animals such as fish use to breathe in water.

identify: To tell what something is.

mammal: A warm-blooded animal that has a backbone and hair, breathes air, and feeds milk to its young.

migrate: To move from one area to another for feeding or having babies.

prey: An animal hunted by other animals for food.

snorkel: To swim using a special tube that makes it possible to breathe while your head is underwater.

species: A group of plants or animals that are all of the same kind.

tourism: The business of drawing in tourists, or people traveling to visit another place.

Index

Websites

Due to the changing nature of Internet links, PowerKids Press has developed an online list of websites related to the subject of this book. This site is updated regularly. Please use this link to access the list: www.powerkidslinks.com/search/whale